FIFTY YEARS IN THE
FERI TRADITION

50th Wedding Anniversary
Victor and Cora Anderson

FIFTY YEARS IN THE FERI TRADITION

by Cora Anderson

Harpy Books
Portland, Oregon

Fifty Years in the Feri Tradition

Copyright © 1994, 2010 by Victor E. Anderson
All rights reserved

ISBN 978-0-9710050-4-4

This book is published by

Harpy Books

an imprint of Acorn Guild Press, LLC

4207 SE Woodstock Blvd # 168

Portland, OR 97206-6267

This book is dedicated to my husband Victor who has stood beside me and helped with the work. Thanks Victor for fifty years of love, trust and pleasure.

Special thanks to Dennis Strand for over twenty years working with us in the Feri Tradition. He wrote the preface for this book and is our special son and an honorable Witch. Thank you Dennis.

Reneé and April for the many hours spent in typing and correcting this book. They are two special Witches who have won our hearts. Thanks for all your work and encouragement. Thanks for all our Pagan friends and initiates that have helped open the way for the Craft to grow.

Foreword

When I was first asked to write this foreword, I was deeply moved. How does one begin to write about a person you have known for almost thirty years, who has taught you their secret Craft, introduced you to the Goddess, given you their personal style and form of charms and Craft tools, set your feet upon a path that would deliver you from false religious fantasies, and opened the door of spiritual perception? Cora has been my spiritual mother and guide, and through the years has given me a love that in time grew to match my true love, that of the Goddess herself.

Her name gives us a clue to her stature, Cora is one of the oldest and most enduring names for the ancient Goddess herself. Since the Goddess is the central figure in Craft theology, possessing one of her names as one's own is in itself a great honor. However, honor is one thing and living up to that honor is quite another matter. Cora has done both.

I first met Cora in 1965 and shortly after that met her husband, Victor H. Anderson. Victor occupied the highest level of Craft understanding and knowledge, that of the degree of Grandmaster. His reputation was, and is still today, based mainly on his authentic practical down-to-earth method of teaching. They were both demanding and exacting teachers, and expecting results, taught me oral and written Craft tradition accompanied with spiritual truths. Their discipline rested mainly on developing an impeccable inner spirituality, which is the foundation of the Feri Tradition. I didn't suspect it at that time but they were giving me another tool simultaneously, the ability to detect spiritual morbidity.

Spiritual morbidity is defined as the deterioration of quality, and when applied to any religious tradition clearly separates and isolates out the falseness that weakens its effectiveness in practice. Keeping yourself and your Craft tools strong, clean and sharp is a test in time of true strength. The effectiveness of any surgery depends directly on the sharpness of the scalpel used.

In June 1973, on Midsummer solstice, I was initiated into one of the Craft's oldest traditions, the Feri, by both Victor and Cora, and through the years continued an ever-growing loving relationship with them both. My Craft wisdom and knowledge, thanks to them, has grown as well. Since our meeting, over twenty-nine years ago, I've achieved some of the highest Craft degrees and credentials that one can obtain, yet I have chosen to remain basically silent and in the background of the greater Pagan community. I teach, but like them, I have become very selective in the type of student.

The Craft, like much of our world today, has become so diversified and fractured by the so-called facts that if a person wishes to become a truth-seeker and solve the mysteries of the Goddess, he will soon become swamped in a quagmire of "facts," misinformation and contradiction. Tragically, this is because most of the so-called Craft teachers are people with lesser insight, and little or no real Craft background, who have indulged themselves in popularity contests or proceeded to make the Craft a business for business' sake. Let's set the record straight, the Craft is not a business! The Craft is in essence the religion of the Gods, an ancient art created by direct contact with them and preserved by tradition, to be treated with respect and caution at all times. Remember the short rhyme: "When conjuring the art of Craft a mist, it's the forces of nature your hands are with."

The Old Craft, as sometimes it is called, has a very dangerous side inherent in its practice. The very forces used are the same ancient ones that set this universe into motion. This major point is too often forgotten, glossed over, never fully realized, or completely realized! Don't forget the powers of Nature's creation include dangerous ones too, like death, disease, pestilence, destruction and deterioration. Nature has her pathological side. So without a basic Craft yardstick by which to measure and separate truth from religious fantasy one is lost, dangerously lost.

Spiritual authority in the Craft rests solely upon the ability of the teacher's art to manifest the Gods, not on a book, notoriety or fame. The authentic Craft teacher will have the distinct talent to put the student into direct contact with the Gods, and as a result create new states of awareness through dreams and visions that open the student to a higher state of himself without the use of drugs or self-denial. Dignity to the self and to sex are held in the highest degree of respect at all times. The student, for the first time in his or her journey, is acquiring that treasured yardstick, which is vital to separating the grain from chaff, truth from illusive spiritual morbidity, dignity from disgrace.

Beware of the Craft teacher who spreads their tradition as if it were mayonnaise or mustard on a piece of bread to be used and seen by all. When I've witnessed this activity in the past, usually hidden motives begin to surface. As time passes that clearly indicates actions as something not Craft at all, but rather a cheap imitation designed and planted to fool the masses and in the long run trash the Craft. The Craft in its pure and more refined states of practice is reserved only for a select few in secret, who have maintained the strongest sense of respect for the ancient powers, laws and the Goddess—not to mention one's own self. Getting the word out and spreading it around is not Craft, but the product of the dangerous tabloid mentality well-displayed by the marketing world today. Such demeanor is usually rooted in, and enhanced by, a false idea of spiritual authority. At first this kind of teacher sounds impressive and, because he's persuasive, probably has a large following, but underneath the thin veneer of surface splash, he as a whole misrepresents the Craft in historical truth, Craft wisdom and tradition.

Cora, on the other hand, has taken another path. Upon reading this book, don't be turned off or fooled by its simple plain hand of language, or the straightforwardness of style in its prose. In Cora's own words, "This book is just plain hillbilly language." On that point I agree, but also wish to mention that the grassroots, hands-on approach of Craft truths that many of our hill people possess has not only preserved a more distinct honest direction to the older wisdom, but also contains within their oral tradition a basically unspoiled core. Cora in her simple old country Craft ways taps this truer wisdom from the source, works with it, and finally puts it down on paper for us all to read.

In our Lady's name,
D. S.

A Woman of Romani Speaks

Within myself I know I am Different,
The blood of the old ones flows
through my veins.
The Gypsies have taught me their magic
And the little people their cunning
I can speak to the trees and they answer
We talk of the moon and the Goddess.
I am told how to plant my garden
And when to gather the harvest.
My lover comes to me when I call
For I know how to live and love
I can teach the children and instruct
the young Maidens
For I have learned how to use my power
And never give it away.

by Cora Anderson

This year Victor and I have been married and working in the Craft for fifty years. As a tribute to him I am writing about our work together, which includes the Feri Tradition.

We met on the astral plane many years before we met on this earth plane, so we didn't need a long courtship. We recognized each other immediately and were married three days later on May 3, 1944. We exchanged our views on the Old Religion. We found we both were Craft people and had Witches in our families. Because of his family and the general public, we kept many secrets. We found that secrets made us strong in our faith. We learned to keep our nose clean and our mouth shut very early.

Victor wrote his poetry, which is a tribute to the Goddess. He perfected it over a period of about twenty-five years. The outcome was *Thorns of the Blood Rose.* Victor is an accomplished musician and plays the accordion. He earned a portion of our livelihood by playing for public and private dances.

Besides working to earn a living we did rituals and worked on experiments and studied the history of Witchcraft. Most of what we found were in bits and pieces from various books including the Bible and much hidden in poetry.

1

In 1945 our son was born. There were many problems with the family concerning his up-bringing. They even challenged his naming. Before he was born I had a dream. A Druid priest appeared to me with a scroll in his hand. He unrolled the scroll and on it was written "call his name Elon." I talked with Victor about the dream. He was very pleased and said that the name meant "Oak Tree." We said nothing until the nurse asked what we wanted to name him. I replied, "Victor Elon." Victor's mother and sister were there. Victor's mother said that Elon was no name and asked me if I would change it. I told her that was his name.

Two months later his sister came to our house. She said the name Elon was in the Bible and she thought it was beautiful. Then I told her I knew it was in the Bible, and that it was in both Genesis and Judges. She was surprised, but ever after to her it was a beautiful name. We did our ritual for him, dedicated him to the Goddess, and asked the Gods to take care of him. He was a good baby. One time Victor felt the devils were bothering him so he put some garlic around the crib. Elon found it and ate it. He really smelled, but there were no more evil spirits bothering him. I made a "love and peace" dream blanket for him, and it really worked. He was a contented baby and slept well at night. We are very proud of our son, he grew to be a wonderful person. He worked very hard for his own education and now is a Health Physicist.

In 1948 we moved to Niles, California. We hoped to find a better lifestyle and more freedom of thought. In many ways it was better, but life was hard and poverty was everywhere. We rented our first house from a Mexican family. They were very kind to us and respected us for who we were. They knew Victor was a shaman and called on him many times. One time a little boy became ill with a seizure similar to epilepsy and looked dead. The grandmother called to us for help. Victor demanded all three of his spirits to return to his body. The child smiled and then began to talk. In a few hours he was playing. The family thanked Victor and told the people that Victor brought him back to life.

We always turned to the Gods in time of trouble. One time we were low on food, maybe enough for a day. We were discussing what we could do. Victor said, "I know what I'm going to do. I'm going to pray." Our four-year-old son said, "Daddy, you can use my drum," which he did. Victor went to the bedroom for his ritual work. I decided to sweep the living room. That house was low on the ground so when I swept the house, I swept the front yard. I was thinking and praying all the time. When I reached the end of the yard my eyes lit on a ten-dollar bill laying in the weeds. There was our miracle, our prayer was answered.

In the fifties we were able to get a few more books relating to the Craft. Victor received a letter from Gerald Gardner and they corresponded for awhile. We could see a pattern forming in the knowledge of the Craft. It was becoming more open.

Victor has always been loved by people of all races. Portuguese, Spanish and Italian all claim him as one of their own. He was often spoken of as a regular League of Nations.

The Feri Tradition

Victor was already involved in establishing the Craft before Gwydion started studying with him. Before the tradition was called Feri, it was known as Vicia, pronounced as in Italian, and *W* was sometimes used instead of *V*, but in Italy *V* was always used. Among Italian Witches the tradition was and still is called *La Vecchia*

Religione (the Old Religion). Vicia is from the language of the tiny slender dark people to which Victor is racially related. The word is the origin of the words Wicca and Witch. Just after the publication of Gardner's first book, Victor received a call from Palermo, Sicilia asking him to establish the Craft in California.

The following is from Victor's own writings: "In spite of the great amount of publicity the Craft has been receiving over the last few years, there is still a great deal of confusion of what is and is not Fairy. I'm sure this is because the word Fairy has been used so long to designate certain kinds of nature spirits. This is not incorrect in itself, but it does mean the more natural and wild forms of human magic and sorcery.

"It was originally applied to a race of very small slender dark people who came up out of Africa as long as ten thousand years or more ago. They spread throughout the world until they reached such far places as Japan, Siberia and Russia. The *Menehune* of Hawaii and other South Pacific islands are the same race as the little people in Ireland and the rest of the Celtic world. Fairy was originally spelled Feri, which means 'the things of magic.' In the Highlands of

Scotland to be *Fe* is to be psychic. In English this word is pronounced like those in Italian, Spanish and Hawaiian. Many of our words are found in languages spoken throughout the world. These include, to mention a few, Old Irish, Highland Scott, Vask (Basque), Native American, Polynesian and I should mention African and Fijian."

The name Fairy became accidentally attached to our tradition because Victor so often mentioned that word in speaking of nature spirits and Celtic magic. In Ireland the people who follow our ways are referred to as Fairy doctors. In our tradition the Gods are not mere concepts but real spirit beings, and are part of the same life-chain of which we and all other creatures are a part. Our Goddess is God Herself. Not only does she have a sex, but she is sex, both male and female. She is the Holy Virgin because she is complete within herself and needs no other. In India she is Kali. Among the Druids she is Mari and Cerridwen. She is the power of darkness and the womb of light. We have a very old saying which is "God is self and self is God and God is a person like myself."

Our knowledge of the structure of the human soul is the same as taught in the secret

Jewish mysteries, and Kahuna of Hawaii and the South Pacific Islands. Read Victor's article, "The Etheric Anatomy of the Human Being." It can be found in the *Société* magazine of Technicians of the Sacred (Vo1.3, No.3).[1, 2]

In Voudou the Goddess is Mawu and also Aida-Wedo. In most traditions of the present time the Goddess is pictured as having one single consort. In what is now called Feri Tradition, she is known to have two consorts. These Divine Twins are exactly alike and can function as a pair or both at once. They are both her son and lover. Among the Druids the first is called Eotates, the same as the Father in Christianity. The second is Esu and sometimes Esus, the primordial savior God from which Jesus takes his name.[3]

In present day Wiccan tradition they speak of the Wintertime King, the Horned God of hunting and death, and the young Green God of fertility, spring and summer as if these were two

---

[1] Address to: Technicians of the Sacred, 1317 N. San Fernando Blvd., Suite 310, Burbank, CA 91504, U.S.A.

[2] This article, along with more of Victor's writings on the subject, can also be found in *Etheric Anatomy: The Three Selves and Astral Travel* by Victor H. Anderson. *Ed.*

[3] See *Merrymount Messenger,* issue #18, page 10.

aspects of a single being. There is nothing wrong with this concept, but the following should be clearly understood. Either one or both of the Divine Twins can fulfill the function separately or together like two candle flames blended into one.

The Goddess conceived and brought them forth, not because she had to have male help, but because in her divine lust she desired them. We humans should be intelligent enough to realize that in the etheric world sex is not a matter of being split into two or more genders as it often is in the world of dense bodies. Though the Divine Twins are male in function they are like all Gods, both male and female in one. They can work as two "females," sexually active lovers, or divine brother and sister, or the divine "male" pair—also sexually active. We could put it this way and say the bright and dark Godhood are the two sides of a chessboard with the Divine Twins at play while Mother makes the rules.

In our Feri Tradition, the male God is also called Melek Ta'us, the great Peacock Lord and Bird of Paradise who shakes his many-colored tail feathers and fills all seven heavens with thunder. Though he is bright, powerful and creative, the Goddess plainly tells us, from under the restraining hand of her love he is the most terrible of all spirits. He is in fact the clitoro-phallic serpent of the Goddess; as with Eve in the story of Genesis and El Shaitan—the name the Christians have stolen to make him into the "Devil." Those who insult his Mother-Wife should keep his displeasure in mind when they abuse sex and throw it around like a baby playing in its own excrement. He is the one who has the scourge, so be warned. This should make it clear that male and female are not two separate things, but two manifestations of the same power and of God Herself. The male is always brought forth from the female.

At this point I want to make a few more things quite clear. In gathering up bits and pieces of the Craft, I did not mean that is our main source of knowledge. I have said that Eotates was the same as the Christian Father, but I am not referring to the false God who is the enemy of Sophia in the authentic Gnostic Mysteries. Christianity worships the same old Trinity as we do. However, they have become a poisonous, sex hating, woman despising, androcentric death cult based on a large package of obscene life negating lies. While telling us we are made in God's image, while insisting that God is a trinity. If we say the soul is a trinity, then we are deceived by "Satan." In their Christian theology, the Holy Ghost is made into a male while their Father and Son walk ahead of her, tending to the "God" business while our ancient Goddess trails along behind, always mentioned last in their male chauvinistic sermonizing.

The idea of one and only one God in the image of a male man is within itself ridiculous. This alleged "God" is worse than any human Hitler. Such a being, who would claim to be almighty, and then base his plan of salvation on deliberate bloodthirsty acts of child abuse, and then condemn all us who refuse to accept it to an eternal condemnation of Dachau and Buchenwald, is not fit for human worship and deserves to be drowned in the blood of his own son. Jesus was a willing sacrifice, as one of many sacred kings who came in the name of his Mother and the dual consort, and not the victim of a vicious bully God made in man's image. So much for catering to the Christians.

There is a saying in the Feri Craft: "There is power in the blood of woman. For it brings forth birth and new life and renews the generation. But to shed the blood of a man is agony and death. Nevertheless, respect the blood of your warriors and sacred kings, which was shed for your deliverance and salvation." If innocent blood be shed by evil priests in wrongful sacrifice the Gods will honor it, even as the earth honors it and brings forth vegetation nourished by innocent blood. *Songa da wo, axe!*[4] At this point there are two books I would like to recommend: *Reinventing Eve* by Kim Chernin and *The Demon Lover* by Robin Morgan.

The Craft as we know it has a code of honor and sexual morality which is as tough and demanding as the Bushido of Japan and of Shinto, which it strongly resembles and in many important ways is identical to. This code is in no way puritanical, ascetic or anti-sexual. Unlike some bastardized forms of modern Wicca, we do not behave like a bunch of slavering mad dogs in heat. To speak honestly, however, like the Arioi of old Tahiti, we are what the missionary would call a sex cult. We strictly honor each other's bonds and commitments, especially those of our women.

---

[4] Translated, it means: "Power and terror of the blood, Amen."

11

Unlike certain others, we do not find it necessary to use offensive language and inappropriate words to describe sexuality, human or divine. Sex is not a doorway leading to something else nor is it a metaphor for so-called spiritual love, but a sun and moon-lit path leading across the sea of life to an infinite horizon. The rock of ages the Christians sing about is really the Yoni (vagina) of God Herself.

At this point I find it important to write about the subject of initiation. I'm very aware that there are many forms of initiation, just as there are many traditions of what we call the Craft. Vicia is a direct survival of old Stone Age religion. At the risk of shocking the self-righteous it is time to speak honestly but briefly about our initiation. From prehistoric times until quite recently the priest of the coven initiated the female candidate by giving her the secret names of God and her consort at orgasm during sexual intercourse. If the woman was bonded with another, her lover had sex with her after which the priest did give her the names. If she preferred not to have sex with the priest, she was initiated by a ritual we call the Intentions of the Heart. After this ceremony her first act of love was honored as part of her initiation. If her lover was not of the Craft, he was treated as an honored guest even if not allowed to witness our secret rites.

There are some important differences in the way the priestess initiates. She usually insists that the male has chosen a lover for his initiatory rite. If she is what we call a Melissa or Bee Priestess she may initiate as the male does. A Melissa is single and quite bisexual. Here I must draw the veil, but I insist that our rites arc beautiful, reverent and truly spiritual as we define that word. If would-be Feri initiates cannot handle this, then they should go to another tradition or risk madness. Victor and I have witnessed many tragic failures of this kind.

Initiation does not make you a full-blown highly trained Witch. In initiation you literally marry the Goddess, her dual consort and the Gods, whether you are male or female. In speaking to her priest the Goddess says, "I love you with the same love with which a mortal woman loves you, but raised to the power of divinity." To her priestess she says, "I love you with the love with which a man or woman loves you, but raised to the power of divinity." Always remember that in the deepest sense the man you love as life companion or in passing is your son, brother and lover and should be treated with love and respect as yourself and other half.

In the authentic version of *Il Vangelo* (the *Gospel of the Witches*) our Goddess Diana says to her consort Lucifer, "You are myself and other half and I place you under the hands of my love." Our real *Il Vangelo* reads far differently than the bastardized version recently published on computer disk. There is no such thing as a Dianic Book of Shadows. The one that has been put forth as such is a blasphemy and an insult to the Italian people. One of the names of Lucifer (Lucifero) is Lucibello, it is made to mean the devil. It really means "light beautiful."

Our Lucifer was never the fallen angel. In Christianity a male angel rebelled against a brutish male father God. In our religion a vile and unclean "male" spirit of a low nature rebels against the most ancient of deities, the Great Goddess (God Herself) and the Father-Son dual consort. He asks her to give him the Earth and her human children yet to be born. When she refuses his proposition he flees back into his lower state in bitter anger. After this he tries to claim all creation as his own and himself as the one and only God.

This false God was never part of the Trinity even though Christianity tries to make him the chief one of the Holy Triad. As I have already said, they tell us we are made in God's image but deny the human soul is a trinity. While Victor has been accused of making this up, this knowledge lies in the heart of the holy mystery teachings wherever found throughout the world. In the Jewish mysteries, which predate Moses and the prophets, the anatomy of the soul was clearly taught. At the present time the Jewish names of the three parts of the soul are *Nephesh*, *Ruach* and *Neshamah*. These are the same as the three souls of the Feri Tradition which is trying to be born among present day Pagans. The three names in Hawaiian are *Unihipili, Ke Uhane Malama* and *Aumakua*. The first two spirits make up that part of the soul which surrounds and maintains the physical body in life and health. The third spirit is the Personal God. She is a female being, but like God is both male and female and can manifest male energy as needed. It can be truly said that the third and highest of our three spirits is God, without denying the Deity any more than we deny the sun by whose light we live. The sunlight falling on our head and shining on the beach where we are at play is still of the sun. Can any of you deny this?

In order to make clear what can be told about our magic, our prayers and our relationships to the Gods and one another, it is necessary to tell a little more of what we know about the human soul. To make this more understandable I shall use three Greek letters to designate the three entities which make up the human soul. I will use the letters alpha (α), beta (β) and gamma (γ) to designate the three parts of the soul as listed above.

The α spirit or soul is the one that inhabits what is called the etheric body or double. This etheric body is more dense than the next two. It is shaped much like the physical body, which it surrounds and partly penetrates. It extends about two centimeters out from the flesh on all sides of the adult human of either sex. It usually appears a misty blue-gray, but is often luminous with a lovely electric pink color. It emits a faint hum like the sound of a bumblebee. In the man it is more feminine than his physical body, and in the woman more masculine. The α spirit is the one who does most of the remembering and creates, stores and uses life force. It is the first to create your passions and desires and even your fears. This does not mean that the other two parts do not do the same, and more so than they usually do as we develop psychically. The α spirit is usually the first to feel sexual attraction and fall in love. In some primitive cultures it is called the bush or animal spirit. The word animal does not put a low meaning to it, but means anima, life soul or spirit. In the ignorant and undeveloped human being the α spirit becomes so full of complexes it can no longer use its form of natural instinctive mentation. In its corrupted state it can drag the rest of its human soul to all the ditches, potholes and cesspools of life.

The β spirit is the one that inhabits the less dense and more luminous body that psychics call the aura. It extends from eight to nine inches from the physical body of the adult human. It seems narrower when viewed from the side, because it is slightly flattened like the body of a paramecium. In children of both sexes the body of the β spirit extends only about seven to eight inches beyond the dense body. At puberty this body attains its full nine inches out from the physical body. The girl is likely to reach the nine inches before her brother does. Victor calls this the auric body. In the woman it is usually wider around the hips than the man. This auric body is the one whose varying colors and tints tell us much about the person we are observing.

The spirit whose vehicle I call the γ body is the Godself. This body is very difficult to see. The γ spirit dwells in the top of the aura. When seen it usually appears like a radiant blue ball of light, sometimes it appears white or gold. Sometimes it will appear nine inches in diameter or less.

Each of these three parts of the soul has a conscious center located in the physical body. The center of the α spirit consciousness is in the solar plexus, the sex organs, and the area in and around the heart. It also uses a center below the navel and another at the base of the spine. The β center is in the head above the nose and between the eyes at a point usually confused as the third eye.

As a rule the γ spirit communicates more freely with the α spirit. This explains why people tend to separate logic from emotion. In most humans the α spirit dominates the right side of the brain and the β spirit dominates the left side of the brain. The γ self or spirit can make equal use of all parts of the brain, but is usually felt more in the forebrain. All three parts of the soul share in the consciousness of our individual selves, but each part can live independently if separated. I realize that this opens a lot of doors that lead to areas I cannot cover fully here. Some of this knowledge is still very secret. Only an ignorant fool would say that we are only as sick as our secrets.

Our tradition is a martial art as deadly as any taught in Japan. Our tradition is not made up of people who keep secrets because we think we are better than others, but because our knowledge is real and dangerous if gone into beyond a certain point. Our tradition of the Craft is not a hodgepodge of mere beliefs, half-forgotten and misunderstood rites boiled up in a cauldron of hearsay that leaks badly at best. We are scientists in the truest sense.

Victor has been accused of making up the pantheon of Feri Gods, Guardians and spirits. He has told everyone again and again that he did not learn all he knows from others verbatim. He certainly did learn much from the people of his tradition, but he is a shaman and priest in his own right. I have personally witnessed his communication with our Gods and have often traveled with him out of body. He has always said, "Perceive first, then determine scientifically what must be believed." In my opinion, based on real experience, my husband is an Einstein of the occult.

Before speaking of our prayers and rituals I wish to state once more that we do not abuse sex. There is a saying among the Kahuna that "the quickest way to create evil spirits in human bodies is to give the pleasures of the Gods to a herd of swine." The Hawaiian word for swine as used here is *pua'a ino,* which means something like "sin pig" and does not refer to animals. Before writing briefly of our prayers and rituals, I wish to make this point very clear. My husband is one of the last Kahuna. Fifty years of living intimately and working with him is proof enough for me that he did not make any of this up. No *haole* upstart has the right to impugn his priesthood and call his knowledge mere beliefs. If any of you who read this could hear his voice lifted in eerie wailing chants to the throb of the *pahu* drum, you would agree that it is enough to strike the fear of the Gods into the most narrow-minded skeptic.

Due to the very nature of his racial and karmic heritage and the nature of the Feri Tradition, Victor is also a priest of Voudou. However, it is stupid to get hung up on labels. There are as many names for the Craft as there are human languages.

The ritual and tools of the Craft are very much alike throughout the world in both time and place. Some of these tools and markings were found in the possession of and on the body of the "ice man" recently found in Europe. Among the ritual things we use in our Craft I would like to mention a few examples. The sacred knife, which has been called the athame, was originally the hunting knife used both for preparing skins and meat, and in animal sacrifice. We use it to raise or to focus power in a way similar to the laser. It was used by prehistoric women like any other such knife was used. It was respected and used as a special object.

The binding cord was and still is used for binding and other martial magic. It is also used in ritual liberation and unbinding. The scourge is used to raise power and in our tradition it is *never* used to strike a human being, even in black magical operations. Scourging is not part of our initiation rites.

When the tools are being given to the new Witch and it is time for her to receive the scourge, the priest or priestess hands it to her saying, "This is a tool of stimulation and raising of power, to strike your enemies, and call up power in the ways in which you shall be taught. It is also your conscience. See that you do not scourge yourself or your loved one." I am not going to reveal the secret uses of the scourge here.

The next is the ceremonial cup or chalice. It is always accompanied by a stone or ceremonial phallus, which may also be made of wax or other substances and is sometimes carved from a root such as a carrot. In certain ceremonies the chalice is held by the priestess and water or wine is poured into it and the priest inserts the phallus into the cup. This is done during the handfasting and the initiation ceremony we call the Intentions of the Heart. In this last-mentioned ceremony the female who is being initiated holds the cup. After which each member of the coven drinks from the chalice in communion with our Gods. The chalice is of course used in other ways. In Huna the cup is made of lava in a cylindrical form and is used in a deadly way not gone into here. The chalice is the yoni female receptacle of the life force (the same as mana).

The chalice and the cauldron both handle the power in the same way. The egg of stone or wood honors the cosmic egg which God held in her womb before it hatched some eighteen or twenty billion years ago in what astronomy now calls the Big Bang. There are other meanings which are quite obvious.

Altars are very simple, but we see nothing wrong with elaborate and beautiful altars holding many sacred and precious objects including God statues and the above-mentioned tools of the Craft. The altar has the same purpose for the Gods as the dining table has for us humans and our families. They both came into being at the same prehistoric date.

Now I would like to write about our ceremonies. The first thing most people think about when you mention an altar is sacrifice. In order to understand what little I can afford to say here, it must be understood that the spirits and the Gods do not have physical bodies as we do. Although the Gods are much lighter life forms than ourselves, we are all in the same family. We can create much more mana than beings having only etheric bodies. The Gods need us and we need them. I can mention three kinds of sacrifice. The first is the shared sacrifice in which we literally eat and drink with the Gods and our ancestors who are sometimes called the Mighty Dead. These are occasions of love and joy even when the purposes are most solemn.

The second is when the offering is burned by fire or otherwise disposed of during or after the service. No living thing is offered in this way while still alive. The only way I can give an example of the third form is an animal that must be killed as on a farm. No such honor is given for animals who die for us daily in the slaughterhouse. Human sacrifice was never a part of religion until men decided to enslave their women and expel them from the priesthood. Very little more must be said here, but I must insist that we do not engage in acts of cruelty in order to raise power. Such religious filth is practiced either by those inverted Christians the public calls Satanists or the self-styled Witches who pass their women around as common property in the name of feminism and so-called Goddess worship. I do not find it necessary to describe rituals in detail. Many such descriptions can be found in literature and by personal accounts.

Only the ignorant insist that all our rituals are handed down verbatim from Witch to Witch. Just as the poet and musician can create great works through inspiration, so we of the Old Religion can make new rituals and services to our Gods. This religion is not a dead fossil, but a living growing human experience. I do not mean to say that anybody can throw any old thing into the cauldron and call it Witchcraft. If people wish to engage in pure filth, let them use their own latrine and leave our traditions alone. A good example of such nonsense is the so-called ten commandments of the Goddess recently published by a self-styled "Elder of the Craft."

Any good ritual must have spontaneity and vitality otherwise it is a mere form like some of the meaningless prattle practiced in fundamentalist Protestant and hypocritically Catholic Christianity. In all rituals power is raised and used in magic operations for the good of our human race, our ecology, or for necessary martial purposes. In every rite each person must be in touch with his or her Personal God. If all three souls are straight within us, we may deal with the Gods as personally and intimately as we do with each other.

Rituals are sometimes called workings. Anyone with any knowledge of the Italian language knows that an opera is a work. We do not want to quarrel with other traditions or their rituals, but we are trying to keep ours authentic. We will never refuse or discard any beautiful rite practiced by another tradition. The real Craft is a democracy, a religion of the common working people and not a set of beliefs dictated by a ruling class. The following should help make the point clear. The priestess or priest must be a gifted shaman and psychic and not like someone depending only on what they have been taught or what they have learned by rote.

The titles Master and Grandmaster apply to persons of either sex and have the same meaning for us as they do in the Japanese martial arts. We always treat them with love and respect.

Unfortunately there are a number of people in the Pagan community throughout North America that insist that Witchcraft by whatever name is primarily a "white man's" religion. Before the Roman invasion which took place in the Old World, the hardy freedom-loving white tribes of the forest were mostly followers of our Goddess religion, with some barbarous exceptions. The real Druids were followers of this religion and would have been the scientists of our present day had they not been plowed under by the followers of the Roman's father God religions. The light-skin people of the great forest were not racist or anti-feminist for the most part, until the tragic invasion mentioned above. This explains why darker peoples trusted the first white people who came to them, not knowing how they had been perverted. The homeland of all the human race is our beloved Mother Africa. When humans left the cradle of their birth on their long walk out of Africa, some were bleached white by cold northern climates while those who stayed at home remained either black or various other darker shades. Then their Christian brothers swooped down on their homeland bringing rape, pillage and slavery in the name of the new God.

Long before this tragic time, Africa gave birth to advanced black civilization, culture and kingdoms. Long before the Egyptian pyramids were built, there was a kingdom then known as the Songe Federation. Their religion was Voudou, or as it is sometimes spelled "Vudu." Its name is derived from *voudou ne* (the way of power). The very small dark people to whom Victor is related also claimed this as their homeland. Whatever their original color, they were quite light of skin by the time they had found their way over most of our planet. They are the same race that lived in Ireland and even the South Pacific Islands. What is now called the Feri religion is much more of the Voudou and Santeria than it is the so-called "white man's way." Those who think it is should visit the woods of Finland, where a beautiful fair-skin people still follow the same faith. Many of the prayers that Victor uses are in the same African language used by what are called "Witch Doctors" in the African order of Sikana of which he is the only light-skin member. Certain racist members of the Pagan community have called him a liar about this, but I have personally seen his work with black people and know it to be true.

The snakes which St. Patrick supposedly kicked out of Ireland were identical to Damballah Aida-Wedo of Voudou. This is not just a head-tripping connection between the serpent of Erin and the rainbow serpent of Mother Africa. The word Damballah literally means "God beating like a heart drum." This great serpent God is identical to the Tiamat of the cultures that came into being later on in North Africa among lighter peoples. She is both male and female and has the dual consort as was described earlier in this book.

The male energy manifested in prayer to the consort Papa Damballah is clean and free from all that is against the female. The Goddess Aida-Wedo is the very heart of Voudou. This energy also shines forth as the male potency of God. The serpent is also Heva Leviathan, which is the clitorophallic power of the Goddess and her dual consort, and the power that is raised out of the earth and the waters and brought down from the heavens in Witchcraft. This mighty force is the dragon of the Orient.

The swastika is also a prime symbol in our religion. The fiendish conqueror who abused it never really understood its meaning. In the Orient it is still honored and called the word of creation and destruction. The Druids called it the word of God. If you doubt its reality as a sign in nature, observe the arms of a spiral galaxy or pour dishwater down your sink and see which way it whirls.

The inverted pentagram is not the sign of the Christian's God of evil they miscall Satan, but the sign of our Horned God. Our detractors like to talk about the sanctity of animal life, but get uptight because the head and horns of the goat, or a wolf's head, is sometimes in the center of this sign.

This brings us directly to another important symbol in our tradition, the Black Heart of Innocence. This sign was worn by young men and women during religious festivals in Dahomey in the days of the Songe Empire. It is defined by this saying which comes from Africa: "How beautiful is the black lascivious purity in the hearts of children and wild animals." The meaning of this symbol has been misinterpreted to mean other things than its real significance, which is purely sexual. As an ornamental sacred object, this may have been the first ornament shaped like the Valentine's Day heart. We are all born sexual beings and unless your heart is still black and innocent do not look too deeply into the meaning of this most holy symbol.

I mentioned two of the requirements for the higher order of priesthood in our tradition, etheric sight and out-of-body travel.

After my husband lost his vision due to an accident at the age of two, he began learning etheric vision both on his own and by being instructed by Mexican Witches. I can personally bear witness to the power of this kind of sight. Just as the eyes of the physical body are used in sight as we know it, the parts of the etheric body I have designated as α, which correspond to the eyes and other centers of perception, are used to see with this extension of normal vision. It is not mere mental visualization but real sight. In learning to use this faculty it is necessary to unify the α and β spirits in healthy normal awareness and consciousness. In Shinto this is called by words that mean "walking the moonlight path." In Huna it is called *Kealaokeike* (the path of the sun). Learning to see in this way takes much training.

Now I wish to write about out-of-body travel (OBT). The simple truth is we all travel when we sleep, but our minds are so cluttered up with complexes and crazy beliefs that we can't work our way out of our own dreams. Any out-of-body experiences which most of us may have are so distorted by dream images that they make little sense when we try to remember them.

When the α and β spirits are united in mutual shared consciousness, then and only then may one achieve fully conscious out-of-body travel. If only the α spirit achieves conscious travel, the waking memory will be more like a dream full of strange images and symbols rather than real perceptions of the astral world. If only the β spirit travels, there can be virtually no memory of the journey upon waking up. However, the β spirit will communicate its experiences to its other half and we will later remember snatches of the experience. Sexual repression, worries and hidden hostilities will keep the α spirit behind in a swamp of dreams.

Sometimes the α part of the soul will take a portion of the astral body and float above you while you are half awake. I have often seen what looked like a transparent image of my own body floating above me. I would seem to go up into it and there would be a falling sensation and my body would jerk as if I had stumbled on the stairs and I would be wide-awake. Ignorance of these facts has given rise to a lot of trashy literature about spirit travel in the astral world. I think it is time to expose the source of this ignorance.

Sexual repression is the root cause of attempted astral travel turning into mere fantasy, more like LSD delusions than real explorations of the astral. The kind of sexual repression I am writing of here is that which is in the person rather than what you do with others. When you really leave your body you will become very much aware of what we call sex-desire on this plane. I am not saying it is something else. What we experience in making love is only a lovely shadow of what we may have with each other in the astral world, which is the true homeland of the soul. In the ancient Jewish wisdom it is said that sex is the foretaste of the worlds to come. The psychically developed human being is able to make contact with the γ spirit of the soul. Only then may we open the door of dreams and step out into that part of nature we call the spirit or astral world as a truly conscious traveler. The γ spirit is the being of light encountered in near-death experiences. When traveling in the normal state of health and consciousness, we learn the truth of another Jewish saying: "To be absent from the body is to be present with God." But be warned—if you despise the body you will lose all the joy and wonder of truly spiritual experience whether in or out of the body.

One of the best examples of true astral travel that I know of is that Victor met me while traveling out of the body. We made love and traveled extensively many times before we met on what we call the earth plane.

What is called the being of light, the γ spirit of the soul, is the true Christ in the teaching of the redeemer God called Jesus by Christians. This explains the greatly misunderstood mystery of Jesus and Christ Jesus. He plainly taught

33

that he performed what Christians called his miracles by the power of his divine parent. This Personal God is the one addressed in the original prayer now called the Lord's Prayer. He plainly showed his contempt for the false God of organized religion when he referred to him as the "God of this world," and ate the *shu* bread that should have been offered to the Personal God. To call the enemy of Sophia "Satan" is a deliberate mistranslation. He should be called what he is, the false God.

What I have written here should help to explain why so many people after near-death experiences think of the being of light as God, Jesus, Buddha, etc. The kingdom of God is not divided against itself.

The wisdom and knowledge which lie at the very heart of our tradition is the same as that cherished by the ancient order of Kahuna. All prayers, rituals and magic workings must include the aid of our Personal God, otherwise we court disaster and madness. Now I will give a few examples of the work Victor and I have done using these methods.

Victor healed a woman of a severe cocaine addiction as we sat around our table. He sat a small bowl of water before her and stood behind her chair. He took several deep breaths, then held his hands over the water and lifted his face upward, expelling his breath in a quick exhalation. He held his hands over the woman's head and chanted a prayer in Hawaiian. He took a small sip of the water and asked her three times "Do you want to be free of this habit?" while warning her if she held back she would receive a frightening shock as if touching a charged wire. She drank the water rapidly and was quite intoxicated for about twelve minutes. She felt very happy and is now free of her addiction.

Another example is the healing of a soldier who had served in the Vietnam War. He came to Victor after receiving a medical discharge. This soldier, whom I will call Jack, had taken part in some terrible atrocities against the Vietnamese people. He woke up one morning hearing his own voice cursing and demeaning him in the worst boony rat language. His agony continued after he arrived in the States. Another soldier who had served in Hawaii told him about Victor's work as a Kahuna. Victor spent hours with Jack explaining the structure of the human soul and how complexes and guilt can destroy us. At times Victor held him in his arms like a brother while Jack cried and confessed his deeds. Victor then said, "Jack I must give you the *kala* service. You have to forgive yourself in a way that includes your Personal God. The Supreme Being we Kahuna call *Ke Akua*, the God, has forgiven you a long time ago. Now it is time for you to forgive yourself." Victor then charged a bowl of water with mana as described above and told Jack to drink it quickly. Jack received an electric shock and was unable to move for about twelve minutes. When he came out of it he was very happy. He said that a beam of pure white light filled his whole being from above his head to his feet and left him pure and free of guilt. He is now happily married and has never heard that accusing voice since.

I hope these examples will show that these three things are necessary if the magic of the Craft is ever to become more than a succession of parties and half understood rituals. These are the uses and understanding of mana (life force), the structure of the human soul in all three parts, and the daily contacts and giving of extra mana to the Godself. If anyone who reads this interprets this as a psychological belief model, you better leave it alone. Kahuna is the most dangerous and deadly form of human sorcery when deliberately misunderstood and abused. The words Feri and Huna mean the same thing.

Keeping oneself *kala* is extremely important in every activity of life. The Hawaiian word *kala* is made of two roots: *ka,* the same as the Spanish *la* (the), and *la,* which means "light." It means to keep oneself clean and bright and free from complexes within and without. These mysteries are understood all over our planet and were at the heart of the human religion long before the isles of the South Pacific were explored and occupied. For a very long time the original Jewish teaching about the structure of the soul has been shamefully distorted and mistranslated from the original Hebrew and its older parent language. At the present time it is very difficult to find any written material on these truths that are the heart of authentic Kabbala. For generations certain Jewish scholars and even Rabbis have been so mesmerized by the idea of one masculine God that they have deliberately distorted the truth, not necessarily through meanness but through terror. In the same way, the original teachings of Kahuna are being twisted and lost by meddlesome people who have no Hawaiian heritage or knowledge of the language. The English word self has a meaning that is different from the Hawaiian root "u" as in *Unihipili,* which I have designated as the α spirit of the soul. The same root letter occurs in the word *Uhane,* which can be the whole soul as well as the β spirit.

Those who are trying to practice our tradition continue to stumble over the word self. To speak of the three parts of the soul as lower self, middle self and high self is really a sloppy translation from the Hawaiian and makes it sound like a moralistic model of the lower, middle and higher self or nature. The magic and science of the "little people" is identical in ancient wisdom and teachings to the purest form of Huna.

Our Craft has many forms of rituals and ceremonies all over the world. We cannot ignore the basic principals of what we call magic and religion any more than we could ignore the laws of physics and chemistry, however different the language and laboratory equipment.

The magic circle and the cone of power are two things that come up frequently in discussion about Witchcraft. When thirteen or more Witches form a circle to raise the cone of power their bodies exude a substance now called bio-plasma in parapsychology. In its denser form it is called ectoplasm by the Spiritualist. This form of etheric matter, which carries a heavy charge of mana, flows out of the Witch's body from his or her genitals, breasts and under the arms. It obeys the collective will of the coven, and forms its base around the circle coming up to a blunt point above the coven members. It is this sub-stance and power which we use in our magic. When viewed with etheric sight the cone looks as if it was made of softly luminous blue-gray mist. We hear a lot of talk these days about grounding the power. As it is done now this practice is dangerous and unhealthy. All the extra bioplasma should be drawn back into the bodies of the coven. In certain parts of Germany this substance was called *geistwasser*. In Ha-waiian it is *aka wai*.

Before the ceremony the Witch should always instruct his or her α spirit to breathe into the body the substance that makes up the cone of power, except that which is set forth in the mag-ic. If the *geistwasser* gets out of hand, it can and usually does raise hell. Each member of the coven must place this living substance un-der the care and guidance of the γ spirit.

Grounding is necessary only if a large amount of the bioplasma is out of control and cannot be put to further use. In this case we give it back to the Earth spirit. Within the body of Mother Earth are powerful currents of energy which are the same as those emitted from the great Goddess Tiamat, whose sign is the great black serpent of interstellar darkness in which all light is born. These telluric currents are a direct expression of the power called Leviathan, mentioned in the book of Job and elsewhere in the Bible.

In the Craft we must literally work with these forces instead of inventing all sorts of fanciful images of the Guardians and spirits which have no relation to their true form and appearance. Practices such as playing with the blue fire as a substitute for the above-described technique have dangerous consequences of a physical, mental and sexual nature. The blue flame when manifested in Craft working must be handled with great care. It is very beneficial, but like nuclear power can be very destructive. It flashes from the athame and tips of wands during ritual practice and then it must be treated with great respect. When shining down from the γ spirit there are only good effects.

Victor and I are confident that the scholars of anthropology of today will recognize that our tradition is older than even the Sumeric and Dilmun civilizations. Some of the incantations I have heard Victor use may be found on cuneiform tablets that are preserved in the British Museum at the present time.

In Eastern cultures the swastika, the serpent and the dragon are all sacred symbols of the mighty power that flows from heaven to earth, from earth to heaven, and within the body of Mother Earth. It is only in the Western world, where patriarchal religion and theology have twisted and distorted human perception, that these symbols have come to represent what they call Satan. We have only to observe the structures of galaxies, whirlpools, DNA, molecules and atoms to read the symbols for what they truly are. Before the Roman rape of the British Isles, the Druids called the swastika the word of God. Many of the monsters in the stories of H.P. Lovecraft are memories of old matriarchal Gods distorted by the fear of male chauvinist mystics. Such cherished folk images as St. George slaying the dragon, or the noble knight rescuing a fair virgin from the clutches of a man-woman sea monster in a dark cave, are but thinly disguised images of man conquering and enslaving woman and robbing her of her power. Although Kathulhu is a real God, this name is really a word for the male potency of the Goddess as Tiamat who breathes life into the watery abyss.

For the benefit of my readers who have a deeper knowledge of our tradition, it should be said here that Kathulhu and Cthulhu are two different words for the above-mentioned aspect of the power of Tiamat. The one beginning with K being also the name of a God.

At the time of this writing it is being said that only an initiated priestess or priest can form circles and lead in ceremonies. This is like saying you can't get together and play music without a professional leader. We do insist that people should not claim Grand Mastership or higher orders of priesthood unless they have earned it.

There are many wonderful ways in which we can all use the things we have learned in practicing the Craft. For example, the best and most natural way is to pray. If all three parts of the soul are straight within, we can deal with the Gods as naturally and honestly as we should deal with each other. We must first learn to make contact with the Personal God. The best example of this is the old Hawaiian Ha Prayer. The word *ha* in Hawaiian means "four" and also "to breathe." In Huna it represents the physical body and the soul in all three parts plus the additional meaning the Native Americans of the mainland give the number. The best way is to breathe deeply four breaths at a time until you feel a tingly sensation in the genitals, tips of the fingers and the head. Turn your face upward and exhale quickly, willing the mana you have collected to flow up to the God. Before this exercise you should consciously instruct the α spirit to store the life force in its etheric body and release it when you exhale. The more natural and intimate your contact with the γ spirit, the more sure you will be with the results of your prayer. You should pray first to your Personal God before trying to contact other Gods. When this kind of prayer becomes as automatic as speaking to your loved ones, it is then possible to commune with the Gods in a loving wholesome way. When you have progressed to this point you should not have to be worried whether you have contacted your Personal God before making prayer.

The real meaning of an ancient piece of advice that is usually written "Thou shalt have no other Gods before me" literally means do not let any person, spirit or embodied, come between you and your Personal God. Such practices as playing with channeling and possession without this knowledge will open the doors to schizophrenia, harassment and possession by vile spirits, and split personality. In real magic it is not "thy will be done," but "my will be done." We are not mere vessels to be used by slave masters. Failure to be integrated as a whole person leads directly to the misunderstanding of karma and reincarnation. Life in the physical body is not just a school of hard knocks to teach us some kind of lesson, but life is to be lived for its own sake, passionately, joyously and normally. Karma is the law of cause and effect and not the combination of whips and chains the slave masters would put upon us. Because karma is a natural law, it is big enough to contain both justice and injustice. It is foolish to believe that every unfortunate condition in life is caused by some sin against others. We all suffer because of things done to us, much more in many cases than from misdeeds in past lives.

An example of this is a regression my husband did. A woman came to him with severe pains in her back and left shoulder. She told Victor that she became very ill when she tried to watch a Western movie on television. When she was regressed, she remembered her life as a man married to a part-Mexican girl. While traveling in Nevada, some outlaws attempted to rob them and threatened his wife with rape. They both drew on the outlaws and shot it out with them. The young man reccived a bullet in the left shoulder and just above the hip. The woman we will call Martha was very attracted to guns, but at the same time had nightmares about gunfights. In all these dreams she was male and married to a Mexican woman. After reliving this episode, the pains disappeared completely. It was also found that the husband was the wife in the incident described.

Another woman suffering from being over-weight and in constant hunger remembered dying of starvation as a child in a previous life. After regression she lost weight and is now happy and healthy. She had been told by several quack psychics that she had been the mother that had starved her child. Victor brings out the point I have made about karma over and over again in his work on regression.

There is another claim often made by undeveloped or fraudulent psychics. They tell us that we all choose the afflictions and misfortunes we are to suffer in the next incarnation while we are between lives. To put it bluntly, this is a cruel lie. I do not mean that no one does this, but that it depends upon the character of the soul whether or not this path is followed.

To give a better understanding of karma it is necessary to reconsider what I have written about the structure of the soul. During incarnate life and in the period between lives, it is the α spirit of the soul that does most of the remembering and keeps the records of these memories in its etheric body. In the case of an extremely wicked life or a very cruel death, the α and β parts of the soul sometimes become separated. In Kahuna this is called *ka mahele* (fission). In the case where Victor healed the soldier who had served in Vietnam, this was about to take place. The author Joan Grant referred to the α part of the soul as the supraphysical body. It is very fortunate when the α and β parts of the soul can remain together life after life, but this is not always the case. When a β spirit of the soul undergoes this splitting off and is paired with another α, the α that is split off will occasionally follow that soul into incarnate life. In our tradition we call this the sin body or the follower. The follower does not have the intelligence of a whole human soul, but has a low animal cunning.

On the brighter side there are followers who are loving and beneficial, having undergone purification after the *mahele,* or separation of the two lower parts of the soul. In most cases the α part of the soul does not remain in that state of development long enough to become a follower. If they remain unpaired to another β spirit they go into a pupa light state, which the Hawaiians call jumping into *po.* After a time they hatch into a β spirit. The Kahuna (or Witch shaman) does not treat the dangerous follower as a Christian exorcist would a "demon." He draws this detached α spirit into his aura of power and occasionally feeds it with mana while winning its love and trust. When it says "I am sleepy" he tells it to dive into the darkness of rest and lets it go. In Hawaiian *po* means "natural darkness," as in night. This should make it clear that the present moralistic and metaphysical nonsense being taught about karma and reincarnation comes out of the wild daydreaming of fraudulent "psychics."

When a female Witch deals with a dangerous follower she must take extra precautions. In case the follower is masculine, and if he comes as a male, he may play upon any sexual aberration or weakness in her nature even if she is not consciously aware of them. He will try to dominate her in the same way a sexually vile man would attempt to on this plane. She must therefore *kala* herself before dealing with these stray α spirits. In order to understand the way we remember past lives, we must keep in mind that the α part of the soul remembers and records memories as described above. The α half of the soul retains all the memories of the complete soul from which it was torn apart and believes itself to be that entire person. It usually has about the intelligence of a smart cat or dog and can really mess up a seance with its childish games. When hypnosis is used as a means of regression by an untrained operator, the *Unihipili* or α spirit will try to please the hypnotist, and especially the rest of its person, with the result that there is much fantasy and very little memory.

When Victor and I regress people we first place the subject in contact with his or her Godself. We do not usually tell the subject what is actually being done, as this might bring up conflicts due to religious beliefs. We find it easier to work with the Catholics, who are more comfortable with the concept of a guardian angel. Any person we regress is always kept aware that they are remembering and not being thrown back in time. A past-life memory is really no different than recalling events in incarnate life. When true contact is made with the Godself part of the soul, she can always be trusted to help the rest of her person find true memories.

This brings us to another question I would like to clarify. As I have stated before, the Personal God though feminine is both male and female in one. Because of complicated religious beliefs most people perceive the γ spirit as a male being. This is especially true in the near-death experience. Obviously, no one is normal when close to death. In this experience male energy is usually required when the soul and body are to be reunited. This explains why so many people say they have seen God or Jesus after coming back to life. To say this is an illusion is cruel and uncalled for. In my husband's near-death experience he saw his *Aumakua* (Personal God) as feminine like God Herself, but also having male potency. The idea that we live thousands of lifetimes only to get dissolved into the Divine is ridiculous. When the soul is ready to leave the wheel of karma as it is on this plane, the α and β spirits of the soul become equal in development, then fuse together like two drops of water to become a γ spirit. This should not be taken as the only explanation of where Personal Gods come from. They existed as our true parents in the etheric region of our planet long before we were created and clothed ourselves with physical bodies in the natural process of evolution. In the ages since then, the life processes have become as complicated as the nuclear chemistry in the hearts of older stars. It is a bit late to look for all sorts of handy-dandy explanations of life's mysteries. The shaman by whatever name must be a scientist, especially in these times.

It is a curious fact that most malevolent followers come on as male. This is because evil exists in two distinct life forms. Positive evil is usually male. Negative evil is usually female. Hardcore feminists get offended at this without stopping to think that we are dealing with evil, which is not expected to be fair and nice. Positive evil is a violent, sadistic, cruel and long-lived evil. Negative evil is masochistic and submissive as well as cunning and cruel. If both manifestations of evil were equal, human society as we know it would be swept away very quickly. Most enduring false religions worship male Gods. However, the older gynarchic Gods seem to stay in the background, but are always with us.

The above material should make clear how necessary it is to have the help of the Personal God in remembering past lives. If the α part of the soul being regressed has been attached to the β part with another set of memories, these are obviously not on the Karmic path of the soul being regressed. However, they are still valuable.

In order to have a better understanding of life between incarnations, heaven and hell, the realm of Feri, and our place in the ecology, we should take a brief look at the structure of our planet in both the physical world and what is usually called the spiritual. There are ten globes in both the visible and invisible structures of our world. One which we are most familiar with while in the dense body is the chemical region. The second is the etheric region. The next seven globes are sometimes referred to as the seven heavens. The tenth is the Kethar or Crown globe. This mystery is best understood by those of us who know the ancient Jewish teachings. All nine of these etheric globes surround and penetrate the solid Earth, which is the planetary nucleus. In most out-of-body experiences, we do our traveling in the etheric region. We see the same things as we see in waking life and much more besides. When we have learned to explore these regions more scientifically we soon learn what conditions in nature have given rise to much of our belief about heaven and hell and the afterlife.

The region we have come to think of as hell exists within the vital or etheric body of Earth. It is not a horrible torture chamber set up by the patriarchal "God" for the torment of damned souls, but a place of purification, recycling and renewal of life forms and energies. To the astral traveler it is a dark, misty and frightening place to be. While it is true that vile souls are often drawn there, it is not a place of eternal punishment, but of purification. This is the origin of the Catholic doctrine of purgatory. To the trained observer doing research into that part of Mother Earth, this realm is as natural as the dark undersea world. The astral traveler can study its native life forms as objectively as a deep-sea diver learns the habits of sharks and other creatures. It is not a Christian devil that presides over this part of our world, but the living spirit of Mother Earth. The life force and vital energies of hell are as necessary to us as the heat generated in the dense body of our planet.

Although the second globe is usually called the etheric region, all of nature above and within the solid planet may be referred to as etheric if we use that word in a way that is not confusing. Immediately above the etheric region and just below the next great globe, is a realm which in our tradition is called the desire world. Whereas hell is usually seen as a dark and murky place, the desire world is a place of brilliant colors and ever-changing forms and scenes. Here both beauty and horror live together. The most beautiful shapes and energies may be seen together with shapes that embody the most voracious and destructive forms of evil. We all contribute and build things in this world. When two evil forms meet they often destroy one another in explosions of many colors as their substance is returned to the material of this plane. If this were not so, our own evil would have destroyed us long ago. This could also be a place from which love, beauty, goodness and advancement could flow back down into our world, but if we would reap, we must sow. In Christianity the desire world is vaguely perceived as the pearly gates of heaven, which in fact it is.

Each of the seven globes above the desire world is made up of seven planes. The fourth or central plane of each globe resembles the one in the globe beneath it. The scenery in the fourth plane of the globe above what is called the etheric region is very similar to what is seen on the solid Earth. The out-of-body traveler will see mountains, trees and other beautiful things seen on Earth, but there are startling differences.

In the chemical region, we are used to thinking of matter in terms of solid, liquid and gas. In the ethereal realms of nature there are seven states of matter. The first three correspond to solid, liquid and something not quite like liquid or gas, but more like coherent plasma. What seems like solid is not solid as we know it. There are forms and structures that when briefly seen may be taken for "earthly" shapes and scenes. The third state of astral matter is difficult to describe. It is hinted at by cloud formations, mists and rainbows in our denser world. If you walk down into a lake in the fourth region of the globe we are describing, it would be more like walking in a three-dimensional image made of light than diving into a lake here. As we move farther out, the central plane of each globe, though similar to the one below, is progressively more ethereal and brilliant in color than the one beneath. The farther out we go, the more incredibly beautiful the forms and colors of these central planes become. The tenth or Kethar world is part of what our tradition calls the God world. This is the realm of the highest cosmic Gods. The God world is the great unlimited interstellar space of what we call the spirit world. We may think of it as the ethereal outer space.

Many people are still asking Victor and I about "the realm of Fairy." So we will drop back down to earth to consider it. The astral world is not some place put here for the sole benefit of humans. It is teeming with many forms of life, including those who are malevolent and dangerous to humans, not because they are evil but because they are different. They are the wildlife of their native habitat. Most of their antagonism is caused by the corruption and destructive behavior toward the environment. In the Western world, the word Fairy has come to mean a race of tiny dark people as well as the nature spirits with whom they live in harmony. In certain remarkable ways traveling in the astral world is similar to being under a tropic sea in scuba gear. To understand this we must once more briefly consider the seven states of ethereal matter. When swimming over a reef we observe solid forms of coral and their dependent life forms. If we accidentally cut our hand the blood will form a red-brown cloud above the cut just before the water takes it away. This is because underwater the states of matter more closely resemble that in the astral world than in our atmosphere.

Among the gypsies of the Colebra tribe, the seven states of the astral are called *rupa* (form) and *arupa* (almost without form). These words are from old Sanskrit. As said earlier, the first three states of *rupa* more or less correspond to solid, liquid and something that is not quite either one, and the fourth corresponds to our atmosphere. It is not easy to describe the last three states, but it can be said that all form exists in an unmanifest way in this high energy matter. An example that illustrates how things look while traveling out-of-body is how a glass of whisky appears when you have floated into a bar. Above the amber liquor a beautiful fragrant gray-green cloud will be seen rising slowly toward the ceiling. The auras and even the breath of the patrons are luminous with several colors.

The realm of Fairy (Feri) exists in what we call the etheric region. The name Fairy applies here to certain well-defined classes of nature spirits. These include the Gnomes who live in the soil and within the body of the Earth. There are several races of these charming little people. I will describe one kind of Gnome here. They look like tiny brown human-shaped creatures with blunt pointed caps. These are not caps but the way their little heads are shaped. They are bisexual, but their sexuality is more like that of young boys with some female overtones. They are sexually very active with each other as they release life force into the soil. They seem never to fly about in the air as freely as the Sylphs and Peris, both of which are spirits of the air and look like a child's idea of miniature angels. Gnomes do move about freely in the earth in all three dimensions like fish in water. The Gnome's average life span is one hundred and sixty-two years. At the end of this time they shed their very earthy etheric bodies and enter into other Gnomes to be born or change into one of the kinds of water spirits. The Gnome's body is very close to dense matter. They reproduce by fission and do not become pregnant through sex, which exists among them for its own sake and to vitalize the soil. This type of Gnome is about five inches tall, but there are other spirits. Gnomes take part in decay and recycling of organic matter, including the dead bodies of animals and even ourselves.

What we call the realm of Feri is not to be tampered with by the squeamish and faint of heart. If we follow the order of the elements: earth, water, air and fire, the next class of nature spirits are the Undines or water spirits. There are many kinds of water spirits. One kind is Hydroni. It is not easy to give them a three-dimensional size, but they usually appear as quite small. They constantly change their shape while imitating the form of aquatic life in their environment. They can even take the shape of tiny mermaids or humans. Like the Gnomes they are sexually very active with each other, but are feminine. Their lovemaking refreshes and purifies the water both in nature and in our bodies. They like to take the shape of any creature that catches their attention including us. If a man sees one she will quickly take his form, but as a female. They appear in several shades of green, aquamarine and blue, and the body color is blue-green to green-blue. They can appear either clothed or nude. Even their size varies depending on what activity they are engaged in.

Another kind of water spirit which appears much larger is the Rusalki. In pre-Christian times, she freely made love with young boys and men when they went swimming in the forest rivers. In Russia and Siberia and other Slavic lands, the shaman associated with them in both love and magic. When the Rusalki takes human form, she appears as a lovely slender green-eyed blond about four feet eight inches tall. In early Christian times the church made people believe that making love to a Rusalki meant death to a man. The name Rusalki was once a name used for the Goddess as Our Lady of the Waters.

The spirits of the air are often called Sylphs and Peris. They are really of several orders. The name Sylph applies more accurately to the small swiftly moving spirits that most Irish children think of as Fairies. In some books there are pictures that are supposed to be photographs of this order of Sylphs. They look like slender delicate human females of transparent silvery color and have wings like butterflies and sometimes like those of a dragonfly. The wings seem less dense than the body. They have always had this shape rather than taking on other appearances. They move more quickly than hummingbirds, so it takes quite a while for one to stand still long enough to be properly seen. They too can become somewhat larger by taking in astral matter and energy which they later give back to the environment. Before it rains, Hydroni rise out of the water to meet these unusually tiny Sylphs, who then change size, taking atmospheric water into their bodies, and make love with them. In this activity both kinds of spirits discharge water back into the air in the form of vapor.

In the fire element there is a class of nature spirits often referred to as Salamanders. We do not know as much about these creatures as we do about the others described above. On rare occasions we get glimpses of them when they are not a part of living active fire. In this state they look like luminous blue spheres about an inch in diameter. When in towering flames of fire they are gigantic as we think of size. For some little-known reason they often take reptilian shapes in the fire, whether in a fireplace or out of control conflagrations. They are not just spirits that live in fire, they are fire which in itself is consciousness. They also appear as fire foxes, fire maidens and fire birds seen by shamans the world over. We must never lose sight of the fact that there are many other spirits who are associated with, and are a part of, what are called the four elements. An example is our fire Goddess Pele who dwells in Kilauea in Hawaii. In Witchcraft we recognize four kinds of fire; coal fire, flame, ark fire or lightning, and star fire as in the plasma that makes up the body of the sun.

The above description of that part of nature usually called the realm of Feri really refers to all the unseen world in nature, but especially those spirits in the etheric region who are most kin to us. It is very dangerous for any person to pry into this kingdom of Feri without a childlike combination of sexual purity and curiosity. The Feri folk resent false pride and false humility. They actively hate the sleazy sexual nastiness and attitude commonly engaged in by a good portion of the Pagan community at the time of this writing. Victor and I have had to deal with women and men who were suffering with all the psychological effects of the misuse of LSD as a result of prying into, and attempting to control, the realm of Feri while in a deplorable condition that can best be described as psycho-venereal disease. We must perceive the realm of Feri with the Black Heart of Innocence or leave it alone. A lot of misunderstanding about this subject has been spread around the Pagan community by certain note-takers who have written about it in a sloppy way and have applied their own version of magical thinking, which is foolish and amateurish at best. One such person wrote in her notebook that the fire Goddess of our tradition lived in a crater in Hawaii. When Victor said our Goddess of fire Pele, she should have understood that with his ethnic background he would naturally speak of her in this way.

The Feri folk helped us in our evolution into humanhood, but we must never forget that we are animals and in many cases far worse than our four-footed sisters and brothers.

I have written this in hopes to clear away the misunderstandings about what is now Feri Tradition. Much of the misunderstanding has been caused by people taking incomplete notes, then when they decide to write or teach they have forgotten what was said and put their own interpretation on Victor's teachings. One example is: Victor said, "The birds are the shadows of the Gods." The person writing wrote, "The birds are the manifestations of the Gods."

Victor is more than willing to teach anyone who wishes to become a Witch. His greatest difficulty in trying to teach the Craft is due to what we call culture clash. Victor's racial and karmic heritage is similar to that of the author Lewis Owens who wrote *The Sharpest Sight*. Both men share the same blend of Celtic and Native American heritage. The difference being that Victor has Apache, Spanish and Hawaiian in the Native American part of his heritage. This really is important and should always be remembered by those who study with him.

To conclude this writing I would like to write a few words about a very special person, Tom Delong (Gwydion). He and Victor knew each other in other lifetimes and both remembered. They also had the same birthday. He worked with Victor on ceremonial rituals and helped in putting *Thorns of the Blood Rose* together for the press. He was a very talented person. He was human and he did make mistakes, but no one has the right to defile his name.

While you are enjoying the fruits of his labors, give thanks to the Goddess he loved.